MAN HUNTING

SECRETS OF
SUCCESS

© GOLDEN RULE PUBLICATIONS

The publisher makes no representation, express or implied, with regard to the accuracy of the information contained in this book and cannot accept any legal responsibility for any errors or omissions that may take place.

Art Director

John Clement

Series Editor

Alex Woodcock- Clarke

Printed and bound by Whitstable Litho, Millstrood Road,

Whitstable, Kent.

ISBN 1 899299 15 7

First published in Great Britain in 1994 by Golden Rule Publications, Eldon Lodge, 52 Victoria Road, London W8 5RQ.

Tel 071-937 3324. Fax 071-937 1137

THE ART OF MAN HUNTING

SECRETS OF SUCCESS

by

A B Crombie

MANHUNTING

This is a guide for every red blooded girl who is searching for a man, whether her ideal is tall, short, thin, fat, hairy, crafted by the angels or constructed like a brick privy with a prominent flying buttress.

You will also find in here a reference to those men that you should not hunt - they are not worth it, and a guide to the men that you needn't hunt - they will find you if they think it worth their while. It is essential for any one who is not blonde, six foot tall, with model good looks and at least a black six figure bank balance. And, let's face it sweetheart, that's all of us except Bjorn Borg.

This small guide is written by an inveterate man hunter, and everything in it has been tried and tested. Not all of the suggestions that follow should be attempted by the fainthearted or weak-bowelled some of them take a lot of nerve because of the possible (but highly unlikely) loss of face.

Hunting a man is like hunting a job - but more soul-destroying.

At first you should look for something temporary, and then move it from temp to perm. To hunt the long term man is unlikely to be as successful or as enjoyable as going on the chase as often as you wish. Of course you may be one of those people who traps her man at first throw, rather like, as a first job cashiering at Marks & Spencers could be the start of a life time career in high street retailing, a seat at Lord Sieff's right hand and as many free knickers as you can shovel into your handbag.

If this is what suits you, think twice. You may have been able to be a famous opera singer if you had been prepared to give up the first and hunt again! On the other hand, it might be that your vocal talents would only ever extend to a musical: "Marge, how much for the Qwikfill Bin Liners?" anyway

There is a certain amount of kit essential for any man hunter.

You will need an accessible and varied wardrobe. This need not be yours, but whose ever you borrow, make sure that the clothes fit, because you should be able to disguise yourself at short notice. A woman wearing clothes that are too small for her will certainly gather a crowd of men - mostly ghoulish bystanders who have never seen woman strangled by her own bustier. A woman who wears clothes that are too large for her just looks like she's dressed by Issaye Miyake which is worse. (Barbra Streisand wears Miyake. This is why, when she recently appeared on-stage in London, she bore such a remarkable resemblance to a Concorde nosing its way out of a large, fluorescent pink hangar).

Another essential is a Wonderbra - this will add whatever nature didn't - and some other decent underwear. A Wonderbra will lift, it will part, it will firm, it will shape, it will mould- indeed, it will do everything that a jobbing plasterer will do except leave white handprints over your bust and charge you £60 an hour for lounging around in your kitchen, drinking your tea. Admittedly, the underwired sections of a Wonderbra do tend to bite into the chest like a toothed man-trap - but, then again, a man-trap is precisely what a Wonderbra is supposed to be.

Other equipment, it goes without saying, are condoms and a toothbrush.

A compass can be of some use as can a tent and carry-mat, but they are not essential (unless you are after an ornithologist).

You will also need some sort of guide (more of this later) and of course this book for general instructions.

Your Rivals

It also helps to keep a pad of paper and a pen handy so that you can jot down any peculiarities in your quarry's movements, and the appearance or behaviour in any rival hunter.

Danger! It is necessary to recognise a rival hunter, though it is not always easy - any good man hunter is rather like a chameleon when she needs to be - i.e. with lizard skin handbag and accessories and a forked and flickering tongue to match. Recognise her and be warned.

In the chase it is perfectly permissible to point out a hunter to the quarry using one of the time-honoured phrases that go something along the lines of; "Look at that tart. You wouldn't think she was forty would you? Why should you? She's fifty-three. The other day she fell off her heels and broke her hair".

You can spot the novice rival by the slightly manic crazed, lab-monkey look about the eyes, the perfect make-up and the leechlike behavioural pattern with which she attaches any respectable looking male in her category. When her man looks at another woman, she is the one who gets drunk and, with mascara running in rivulets down her face, dances on the table with her skirts over her hips at the most unsuitable occasions, like the minute's silence on Armistice Day.

Old hands are much more dangerous - not least because of their long, blood-red painted nails (Why do older women go for this? Don't they know they could put someone's eyes out with those things?).

They have a way of hypnotising their victim and inveigling themselves into the poor man's life until they become a familiar, long-term feature of his life - like an ulcer.

Disposing of the rival

Sabotage one of her heels (3-1 oil works a treat. There's nothing more gratifying than seeing a rival attempting a graceful entrance at the top of the stairs, dressed to kill and festooned with jewellery, and then watching her slip and cartwheel into the band, twenty feet below, just like Norman Wisdom but less funny, if possible).

Slip a positive NSU report into the top of her handbag (if you don't know what that is, ask a doctor), or a pamphlet on "Living With Discharges".

Send out rumours that she kicks with the other foot (and no, I am not referring to her tryouts for Celtic FC).

Fill her name in the coupon for a home visit from the double glazing salesman on the evening she has arranged dinner a deux at home with her beau so that a stream of bright young men with biros in the top pockets of their shirts turn up on her doorstep every quarter of an hour.

Simply saying to your man: "My! Doesn't she look just like your mother?"

Don't whatever you do think that you'll put him off her by disparaging her moral standards. There is nothing that enlivens a man's interest in a girl - even a real old boiler - like being told that she is anybody's. He will start to preen and try to catch her eye. You will almost hear him thinking "Hm. Anybody's eh?"

MAN HUNTING - THE BASICS

A certain amount of brazenness is useful, but it is always important to know when to use a more subtle approach. After all, more love has been made to sobbing violins than the oompah-oompah of the band of the Royal Marines.

Make-Up

Always be careful about wearing too much make-up. Women who wear too much make-up always have an impassive, slightly laminated look like a Cyberman from "Dr. Who" or Ronald Reagan during his second term.

The effect you want to achieve is the freshness of an oil painting rather than a triumph of the embalmer's art.

Anyway if your manhunt is successful your make-up might smear. So always use cosmetics labelled:

"This lipstick has been tested on animals". If it works on a caged beagle pumped up with steroids, it can certainly stand up to Barry from Accounts, however many lagers he's taken on board at the office party.

Panties

Always make sure that your seams are straight, your bra strap doesn't show and, if you are wearing knickers, that you have no VPL. You are, after all, going into battle - and before you go into battle you must always gird your loins. But it's difficult to sit down without a ripping-sound if your loins are too girded.

The Hunting Grounds

Each man has his own habitat. Having decided which type of man you wish to hunt, it is in his own patch that you will find him.

The fern bar.
The library.
The record store.
The park.
The wife's funeral.

**The Kop end of the football pitch.
The maximum security prison.
The Monkey House at London Zoo.
The gutter...**

...You can find them anywhere.

Species

There are many different species of man and you must make your choice of prey quite carefully.

The methods of luring your prey can be very different, and it is a waste of time, effort and very probably funds to use the wrong type of bait. For example, the seventy-five year old Fellow of All Souls is not likely to respond to the "Oooh! Dun't champagne make you feel all tiddly?" ploy while the nineteen year old playmaker for Manchester United will only grunt non-committally when you say: "Of course, in terms of pure muscle density, the average football player is less fit than, say, this fellow you call 'Giggsy'".

And dress accordingly. If you walk into the Hayward Gallery wearing a spangly boob-tube, white pumps and a Bet Lynch-style four-and-half foot beehive, you are more likely to be applauded for making a daring post-ironic statement and sold to the Saatchi's for £20,000 rather than getting off the curator. And entering the locker room of any team in the Five Nations Championship dressed as Jo Brand will get you burned as a witch.

Butts

If you are not sure which type of man you wish to pursue, cruise for a while and see which style of butt takes your fancy.

Here is the butt checklist:
Is it firm?
Is it shaped?
Is there visible muscle tone?

Is it, at one end of the spectrum, a tight, taut, walnut-cracking butt of the Will Carling-type or is it, at the other, the 60 lb-of-loose-porridge-in-two-saddle bags type as favoured by Kenneth Clarke?
Does it begin to talk after its owner has enjoyed a bean supper?

Having decided on a variety, use the relevant tactics in the right environment. You will probably find a great deal more butts in similar style when he is in company (and therefore more choice - you should not at the start of your manhunt have your eye solely on one specimen - they all have their merits). Most breeds of man tend to hang out in packs, and it is worth looking at a whole pack before choosing a single specimen. There are, of course, certain varieties of man who prefer their own company to that of their peers, which diehard man hunters refer to as the lone wolves or lone rangers. They are more of a challenge to lure rather than to catch, but not necessarily worth the effort.

More of this anon.

GREAT PLACES TO MAN HUNT

If you are not sure what you are looking for - start with an open mind and shop around. Hang out for a while.

Shopping

Late night food shopping is ideal. You can tell what sort of man you have in your sights by the sort of food he has in his basket.

The man who buys real food which he is then going to have to cook may not be ideal. He will probably be a better chef than you, and you cannot tell how many people he is preparing for. Beware that single steak may well be going into a stir-fry for Salt n'Pepper and their entire wide-hipped posse.

Far better to choose the man with a single pizza and a bottle of Chianti in his basket.

Approach with caution - you must not scare your prey. Discuss anything - the lack of choice; the abundance of choice; the proximity of the local pub; the howling outside at the full moon. Improvise! Check out together and walk in the same direction as him. Offer to cook his goose. He can only say "Yes" or "No" and what have you got to lose? If it all goes wrong, find another supermarket or shop at a different time of day. Or slip a Mars Bar into his coat pocket as he leaves the shop, then call over the store-detective.

The Golf or Tennis Club

Both types of clubs have big advantages in that not everybody is accepted as a member. Thus a certain amount of butt weeding has already taken place. Be careful, your particular taste in derrieres may not be catered for at every type of club. At the Darlington Gentlemen & Unionist Dart Club, they are very much in favour of the Brickie's Moonrise type of butt.

However most club committees deserve a lot of thanks form a true man hunter for doing this arduous task for you. Tread cautiously, though - you may find yourself faced with a bunch of red faced, bewhiskered true-blue home county Tories. If this happens, start again. This type of man is only worth it if you have him stuffed and mounted as you would do to favourite pet - not mounted and stuffed as would be done to you by your favourite Chippendale.

Tennis is possibly the sexier of the two games, and shows you at your better advantage. After all you can wear frilly knickers and very short skirts and your partner will think you are well dressed for the occasion. Get yourself involved in the club tournament, and only ever lose to a good looking man. He will feel honour-bound to buy you at least a drink afterwards.

The cutest people you will find in either club, though, are the coaches. Remember that your back hand swing is what you need the most help with, and ask for it to be demonstrated to you physically. To prepare for this clasping-squeezing experience, have a friend practice the Heimlich Manoeuvre on you first.

Book Shops And Libraries

If you are not sure what sort of man you want, but you are interested in a certain subject, then these make perfect hunting grounds. Hang about the area of your favourite subject and discuss the merits of any book with any man who comes along.

Be sensible, though. If you hang around the Airfix Modelling Manuals or "SAS Guide To Piano Wire Strangulation" you are going to find yourself a real weirdo whose hobbies probably include clocktower sniping.

And do a little research first. D.H. Lawrence was not the one who rode across the desert on a camel with Omar Sharif, "Bleak House" is not the "Judy Finnegan Guide To Home Decoration" without pictures and "Learn To Love" in the Reference Section is less likely to be a sex manual than volume xii of the Encyclopedia Britannica.

The Car Park

You can tell a man by the car he drives. You can also tell a man by the place he parks. Never let anyone tell you different.

Find yourself a reasonably smart car park and hang around the smarter cars. A distressed look and - "What have I done with my car? Oh Dear, Oh No" will probably get you a lift in something very comfortable - even if it is a closed police van while a stony-faced plain-clothes DCI quizzes you on the surprising number of Porsches that have been disappearing in the area.

Most men of all breeds have a fascination for cars, so if you decide that the first driver is not really your type, try the next. You will soon find the variety that suits you best. Why make do with a Hyundai Pony when you can have a thoroughbred Mustang?

The Theatre

Theatre provides a much better backdrop for a good hunt than the cinema.

Men do go to the theatre on their own, but cinema is much more social. You will be put off by the horrible wet sucking sounds of the thirteen-year-olds snogging in the backrow, the showers of pocorn from their ten year old siblings in the balcony and, most of all, the seveteen and a half foot wide smirk of Bruce Willis as he thrusts a serrated hunting knife into the guts of the bad guy on screen. No woman is at her best in these circumstances.

But a man sitting on his own in a theatre bar during the interval is just asking to be hunted. He will probably want to discuss deep and meaningful aspects of the play in progress. This can be very boring. Make sure that you have some prior knowledge of the play in question, with one or two impressive quotations from critics or fellow playwrights. This will intimidate said victim and if he does not offer you a drink within two minutes, he was not worth the trouble anyway.

If he says: "During one of the pauses in Harold Pinter's "Mountain Language", I met a girl, went out with her, moved my stuff into her flat, broke up with her and re-located to Cardiff and still got back in time before the next person spoke" you will know that you are on the right track. Reply: "Yes, the same kind of thing happened to me during one sentence spoken by a character in Tom Stoppard's "Arcadia". Except I also had time for a round the world trip to forget".

DIFFERENT PREY

THE LAD

The lad, or one of the lads, tends to be a creature of habit. Nasty habits too. Like the marathon pub crawl, followed by exhibition doner kebab juggling and completed by the seven yard sprint to the toilets.

He sticks with his peers and behaves not necessarily in the way that he wishes to behave, but as his peers expect and encourage him to behave. There are different types of lad.

THE PUB LAD

You will find him with his mates after work only having five or six pints on a Tuesday because it is a work night.

Pub lads tend to become reasonably wide in girth as the years go on, smoke reasonably heavily (but nothing illegal), and look more and more like their companions - red, round, soft and covered in tatoos.

Only their Rottweiler could love them. You should be aware of this fact when you start the hunt - it is important to see the potential growth of your victim in all directions.

A pack of lads can be quite intimidating as a prospect, and reasonably hostile to the hunter. The particular specimen that you select as your prey will be egged on to behave badly by his companions, or teased mercilessly if he does not conform. The "lad" out of his own territory, and without his brothers in arms always considers himself soft and sweet and misunderstood. When he is out of their company, he is also at his most vulnerable.

A bunch of flowers will probably go down better than a six pack of lager - he would prefer the six pack but still likes to think that he is a romantic at heart, and anyway he can always pass them on to his mother if he doesn't know what to do with them. His model of a stable family relationship is that between Grant and the singing pig from "East Enders" (ie. extreme violence with shot-guns punctuated by boozy bouts of begging for forgiveness).

Remember, though, that if the flowers are intended to lure him away from some sort of current entanglement, he will not only appreciate the gesture, but will probably pretend that he bought them for your rival. One way of getting around this is to make sure that they are together when the flowers are delivered (but make sure that they are anonymous in this case - otherwise you will have not only have exposed him, but will have revealed yourself to your rival - bad move).

The bolder approach is to attack him in his natural habitat. You will have to learn to play pool very well, so well in fact as to look as though you haven't a clue what you are doing. This is known as the "Hustle". If he loses more than £20 to you after your first cannonball break, the whole deal will be off.

During your hunt, your ears will be assaulted with bad language that would make a sergeant in the Paras give a little cry and swoon. Don't join in. You do not want to become one of the lads, you are just trying to charm one of them out of the pack. Lads tend to like their girls petite, giggly and feminine and seeing one of the them turn into a Tasmanian Devil with the vocabulary of a twisted gynaecologist will cause them to spill their beer. Causing a lad to spill his beer deemed a mortal offence in all laddom.

Spilling your own drink, on the other hand, can be a vote winner for you. It's easy to engineer - just corner him and wait for someone else to nudge his elbow or perhaps get him to describe how he has fuel injected his Capri (lads, not the most articulate of the higher mammals, cannot describe any object more complex than a single-celled bacterium without using his hands. Asking him, for example, to describe a spiral staircase will cause such a flurry of wild hand-movements that he will take-off like a helicopter).

Pouring beer over yourself, surreptitiously, will bring you to his attention, which is the first objective of any man hunt. Dramatics and charm at this moment will go a long way; dramatics by themselves not. So screaming your head off and attemtping to clock him with your handbag is undiplomatic. The only response you'll get is a shove into the cigarette machine and curt "Shut it slag or you'll get a good glassing" when what you're looking for is: "Sorry luv. Oi, Desmond, a large Kahlua for madame. In a pint mug".

If this ploys doesn't work, then you will spend an unpleasant evening feeling a mild and bitter (assuming mild and bitter is your tipple).

Asking for a light is a simple way of making the first introduction to conversation, but asking for a cigarette is not a good start - men tend to resent being asked rather than offering first. However, asking for a cigarette in return for a drink is a sure fire way of starting something. Your approach will have been bold enough to have been recognised, and challenging enough to be accepted.

Don't try this if you don't smoke. You'll turn a sea-green colour, the room will swim and, inevitably, you'll throw up. This will be especially off-putting for the lad if you do so in the back of his motor. A lad's girl always throws up in her handbag.

Where to Look

If you are anxious to find your lad, and are not quite sure where to start looking, you need an idea as to where to start. Lads are to be found in not-so-smart pubs in city centres and snooker clubs. It is not really worth buying a special guide to such places, but just hold your nose in the air and whiffle a bit. Follow the smell of black and tan.

What To Wear

Tight jeans and a boob tube if you can face it. If not, take your Wonderbra out for a walk, but try to look as if you've left your brains at home. Hairspray is essential. Wearing a perm will help you fit in to your environment.

Possible Problems

Drunkenness

To avoid this, it is best to arrive in the pub before pub lad will have got through more than four pints (ie. forty seconds after he's swaggered through the swing doors). Otherwise he will be pouring either his heart out to his next door neighbour or his guts out in the loo. Whether you get lucky or not, he won't remember in the morning.

Aggression
Do not talk about Spurs in Highbury or Arsenal in Tottenham. Try to keep off the subject of the Irish problems in Finsbury, or supporting the BNP anywhere. Don't mention the M11 in Leyton.

Pick-Up Lines

"So which type of bitter would you recommend for a sweet little girlie like me"

"Was it you who just dropped this fiver, or was it just a lucky find?"

"Can I buy you a drink?".

THE CITY LAD (or ESSEX LAD

To be found, obviously, in the City or in Essex.

There is a certain amount of cross-over between the city lad and the pub lad, but the city lad tends to look after himself a bit more.
He is the original wide boy but supercharged by a

high octane salary. His threads tend to be expensive, or at least that is what he aspires to. When buying a cheapish suit, he will try to look as though he is buying Georgio Armani. Look at the label: Next for Men.

His tie will be brightly coloured and is usually recognisable as something famous, Gucci or Hermes. This is his version of mating plumage and you are not to spoil the effect by saying: "Gosh, a bird seems to have dumped on your shirt-front".

City lads are very pleased with themselves - only a Scotsman with a grievance or John Selwyn Gummer is more bumptious. Indeed, they can be very good catches - they earn really silly money and need someone to spend it on. They think they are gorgeous, and being complimentary to a lad about his build will normally be taken as a true fact rather than a general compliment. A comment on his haircut will elicit some stupid response like "Cheers - I had it done Tuesday when I was down for my daily shave at Trumpers. Cost me £45. You pay a little more but you get what you want". He will not turn to you and say "I like yours too" because hair is not what he will be concentrating on. (Oh, and when complimenting him on his tonsorial investment, better not say: "And how clever Mr. Trumper was to make bricks without straw" because balding city types are very sensitive. It's the pressure of sitting at a Treasury work station screaming bids into three different telephones as Sterling falls through the floor that does it).

It is important to make physical contact as soon as possible, as that will make him identify you amongst the other hunters around. A line like "What a wonderful tie, who's it by?" and then grabbing it seems to work well. It is not only complimentary to your victim's taste, and therefore to yours (even if you did lie a little), but has the symbolically powerful feeling of pulling him by a rope. It also has the added advantage that you can see who really did make the tie (assuming that he can't sew too well, and that he hasn't changed the label), and if it is not expensive enough, find another victim. (Otherwise sling the tie over the nearest rafter and tug hard - there hasn't been a lynching in Oriels or the Pheasantry for quite a while).

N.B. If you really feel that you cannot face telling your victim that you like his tie, use the same tactic, but tell him you hate it instead. This will give you the opportunity to give him a tie as a present (Cost - £50.00) in the future. Make sure that it is suitably laddish, and when he is grabbed by another predator, he should have the decency to say where he got it from.

Other essential things to find out about your Lad are the type of car he drives, where he lives and with whom. If the answers are Maserati Bi-Turbo; South Kensington; on his own, then you are onto a winner. If they are Mum's old Peugeot 305; Leyton; with his sister - find another victim. He is far too ordinary, and besides, sisters can spot a man hunter miles off.

What to wear

City lads tend to be aggressively interested in bottoms, breasts and legs in no particular order. If you accentuate the best of these three options, in your own particular case, it is unlikely that City lad will even notice that he is being hunted, and will think he is the one who is in luck. It is important to look quite expensive, though, because money is all he understands. A pair of really good leather jeans will stand you in good stead, as will good perfume and expensive highlights.

Where To Look
You can find a city lad in any watering hole that serves large quantities of expensive booze (remember that this is vital to him, rather like the Japanese) in the city, but it is worth looking at more than one place - each lad settles to his own level, with the most laddish lads hanging out in the bar at Quaglino's and the Caprice.

Problem areas:

Drunkenness:
You must find your lad before he has drunk two bottles of champagne, because otherwise he will be being unutterably rude and pompous to his next door neighbour, or will be lewd in the loo. Either way, if you get lucky, he'll blame you in the morning.

Aggression:
Do not talk about Mercedes to a Saab driver, or Coopers to a Morris driver. Keep off the subject of liquidators and bankruptcy lawyers. Don't bring up the subject of drugs - that winds them up properly, and for God's sake don't question the cut of his suit. It cost him a fortune.

Pick-Up Lines:
"Which of these fine Australian wines would you recommend for a chic young bimbo like me?"

"Did you just drop this £50 note / gold card or was it just a lucky find?"

"Do you want to buy me a drink?"

THE INTERLLECTUAL

The Intellectual is easy to identify. He has an old battered briefcase, perhaps a pair of unfashionable glasses, a penchant for wearing corduroy trousers that have seen better days and a tweed jacket with leather patches on the elbow. His hair is dishevelled and parts in the middle so that two wings seem to rise and fall down the side of his head - cf. Hugh Grant's hair-do in "Four Weddings & A Funeral" in which the effect of a crow having come to rest on the top of his head to die is superbly realised.

There is almost invariably a book in the outside jacket pocket. Hunting an intellectual can be very rewarding - if you find one with a sense of humour, you will be able to repeat his ideas, without attributing them, when he isn't there, so that your friends will think you have become an expert in some field. Without the sense of humour, you will never remember what he has said. If the worse comes to the worse, you can always steal his books (Goethe said that "Books were the stepping stones to wisdom" and, if you've got enough of them, they also make a very good step-ladder to the top shelf of a tall drinks cabinet).

Know Your Subject

There are major problems with hunting most intellectuals, however. They (pre)tend to be too unworldly to notice the effect of the Wonderbra, and you really do have to know something about something to gain their interest. Pick your subject carefully. Let it not be "English" or "History", subjects so broad that they take a lifetime, well, more than an afternoon, anyway, to master because it's so easy to make a mistake and there's nothing more humiliating than having your first serve contemptuously swatted back over the net, almost absent-mindedly, by the intellectual with a stroke along the lines of: "Actually, Jane Austen never wrote a book called 'Pride & Pregnancy', the Battle of the Bulge is not a new video by Mr. Motivator and the General Theory of Relativity will not explain who married whom in 'Neighbours'".

Make sure your subject, too, is worthy of your quarry's interest. It's no use devoting a lifetime to getting yourself a doctorate in "Applied Lipsticks" or "20,000 Ways To Get Out Of A Mazda Showing Plenty Of Thigh But No Knickers". He just won't care.

Choose a subject, interesting in itself but about which he won't know much because it's so specialist. Perhaps: "Sexual Positions As Practised By Tantric Monks, 1840-43" or "Interesting Ways Famous People Have Died" (with special reference to Catherine the Great) or "The Wit & Wisdom of John Major".

Where To Look

Intellectuals have an annoying habit of working at home, so that a congregation of intellectuals can be difficult to find. Perhaps you might gain entry by pretending to be a computer specialist. All intellectuals have to work with word processors these days but, despite having brains the size of a planet, when something goes wrong with the little glowing box, they can do little more than dance round it in ever decreasing circles like headless chook, crying "My, oh my! However will I get my thought piece for the Sunday Times on the Super Information Highway finished now?". This is when you appear and suggest that the little box might work better if it was plugged in. They are clever, these intellectuals, but not bright.

It is, though, quite possible to find them - they all have to do research for their work. There are a number of pubs and cafes very close to the British

Library, and a lofty and loud conversation with a friend will normally draw them out of themselves. If you have already decided on your particular victim, find out what his subject is, and, whatever it is, hold this loud conversation on a close subject. He, being brilliant (of course), will come to tell you where you are right and wrong. Listen, and after a few cleverly placed questions with nice long words and you will have lured him. (Words to include; "Serendipity", "Semiotics", "Fouccault", "Bimetallism" and "Islets of Langerhans". Words not to use; "Oi", "Shut it", "Four-Eyes").

For this to work, though, you have the small and insignificant problem of learning enough about his subject. This takes time, a high IQ and patience, and if you decide in the end that you would rather go hunting again, you will have filled your mind with a lot of useless information. It is probably faster and more satisfactory to use the direct approach and offer to sew on one of the missing buttons on his jacket.

THE PSEUDO-INTELLECTUAL
Pseudo-intellectuals are much easier to hunt. Play

them at their own game - argue with them (but never prove them wrong - you must remember that man believes he is the master of the master race); agree to disagree over some matter and also agree to continue the discussion at a later date. Since he is a pseudo-intellectual, you are able to be reasonably ill-informed and your arguments can lack logical progression. He will never notice - his will be worse.

To tell the difference between an intellectual and a pseudo-intellectual is not always easy, but a sure fire way is to check the papers and books he says he has written. Membership of the British Library is no guarantee, as all pseudo-intellectuals worth their salt are members as well, once they have left University. If he has written a book based on research - Christian Martyrdom in Indonesia , 1874-1875, he may well be an intellectual (but very dull), if the book is about the psychic reasoning of time, or man hunting, you can be fairly sure you are looking at a prize bullshitter. Always beware of poets - it is very difficult to tell which category the poet fits into, but whatever they think of themselves, the pseudo bracket is more likely. These days, poetry is just about writing prose and re-arranging it to look right.

Ode On The Decline of Poetry

Always beware of poets -
It is very difficult to tell which category
The poet fits into,
But whatever they think of themselves,
The pseudo bracket is more likely.
These days, poetry is just about writing
prose
And re-arranging it
To look
Right.

...See what I mean?

What to Wear

This is another great way of telling the difference between the true academic/intellectual and the pseud is the disguise to which they are attracted.

Surprisingly the intellectual prefers a touch of subtle glamour on his arm. After all, he is not going to find much of it in his study is he? See the joy light up in his eyes as he looks up from his lives of the dead poets to see a live fox in a drop-dead basque and not much else. Names and labels don't mean much, but stockings and suspenders do.

A pseud, though, is another story.

He never gets it quite right, and prefers the student look. Long ethnic skirts, long, lank black hair and the complexion of moon ripened cheese are considered ideal. Study old episodes of "The Addams Family" to get the right effect - Morticia has perfected the look (though touches of Uncle Fester will add nuance here and there). There must always be the possibility in your dress and manner that you are quite capable of taking an overdose and being found with his photo between the leaves of the copy of Sylvia Plath's "The Bell Jar" that will be found in your lifeless hand.

See what the Oxfam shop has to offer, or borrow something that your mother wears in the garden. He'll never know what hit him.

Where To Look (Advanced)

If you find nothing that interests you in the environs of the British Library, or London seems a little far to travel, you could try the libraries of any of the major universities. Forget the red-brick universities, though - they are always far too earnest, and still searching for their place in life. A warning to anyone who gets fanatical about intellectuals; steer clear of All Souls, Oxford - once they have got that far, they tend to have forgotten why they were born with three legs.

Problem Areas

With the intellectual, the main problem you are going to have is looking stupid.

There are few more embarassing things than forgetting your lines - and muddling misanthrophy with philanthropy, meritocracy with mediocrity. Besides, if your intellectual falls for your original act, you may be stuck with having to show your none-theless charming ignorance at some stage "I always thought Montezuma was a type of tequila".

Having hunted the intellectual, you will always have

to be boning up on his subject - and there is nothing worse than having to put your brain into gear first thing in the morning.

Of course these problems do not occur with the pseud. He will think that Montezuma was a type of tequila and coca and cocao are one and the same, but you might get a little weary of playing with his ego.

Pick-Up Lines for the Intellectual:

"Which of these Virginia Woolf books would you recommend?"

"Is that your copy of Jean-Paul Sartre, or is it just a lucky find?"

"Will you autograph this copy of your book for me?"

"Why don't you explain deconstructionism to me over a cup of coffee?"

Pick-Up Lines for the PseudoIntellectual

"Which do you think is smarter, reading a book the way you are holding it, or the right way up?"

"Is that your copy of Asterix in French that has just fallen to the floor, or is it just a lucky find?"

"How about a nice little Caffe Coretto?"

"Will you autograph this copy of somebody else's book for me?"

THE LAWYER

A lawyer is always a good catch, though he, like all men, will have his draw backs.

He will obviously be bright and clever, though he will be pedantic and pernickety.

He will also eat human flesh.

When he hears how an articualted lorry has jack-knifed into a transit van full of kiddies on the M25 he will not say, "How tragic". His ears will prick up, his nose will become wet and he will stand, quivering, with one leg raised, like a Red Setter who has scented game or, in his case, a legal holocaust with damages galore.

The greatest advantage of all is that, if he is any good as a lawyer, either as a barrister or solicitor, he will not only be very wealthy, he will also work extremely hard and for very long hours. This means that he will leave you with plenty of spare time for hunting other types of men on his funds. They do go in a bit for pre-nuptual agreements, though, and you must absolutely refuse to sign ("But darling, I'se just too stoopid to understan' what this long an' squiggly docment means. Does it mean oo doesn't love me any more?"). If you do sign then you are cutting yourself off from the pleasures of man hunting in the future, and you should never put an end to anything that is quite so enjoyable.

There are better ways of finding your lawyer than hanging around the court rooms or the magistrates' offices. Instead of stopping a solicitor, you might get stopped for soliciting. Actually this can be useful, they can always do with a good brief, and you will actually meet the man you had your eye on. Better, though, not to have your intended victim think it in any way possible that you might have committed a crime. Lawyers do not think it is very good for their image to be caught consorting with possible criminals and, besides, being stopped for soliciting outside a court is a little too close to home it's about as bad as outside a police station.

If you find yourself on a jury, you will have the pleasure of listening to a barrister, who will hopefully be a man, for hours. If you are very lucky he will be young and agile. The only problem is that you are not allowed to communicate with him. The ogling can be fun, though. It is not done to burst into applause every time your favoured advocate rises to his feet, nor shout out "Good question. Ask him another. Everyone can see he's lying" when he first approaches the witness and, when your boy is prosecuting, it is certainly innappropriate to return from the jury room having swung a guilty verdict with a recommedation for the death penalty when the accused was only charged with removing from a mattress one of those labels which reads "Removing This Label Is Against The Law".

Getting yourself arrested for a crime you couldn't have committed is a great way of meeting your lawyer. Ring the police and shop yourself anonymously for a crime that you have not committed, and then dress in your best Armani jeans and for Christ's sake look sexy. Lawyers are nothing if not blind to subtlety. When the police come to arrest you, look shifty and bewildered, but go with them. The first thing that you say in the police station is that you will say and do nothing until you have a solicitor present. Then ring the solicitor who is your intended victim and tell him there has been a terrible mistake, and please could he come and help. At some point during your time alone with your victim, you tell him that you always wanted his body and this was a silly trumped up charge - you couldn't have done it because you were at the beauticians having your tummy button pierced. He will then get you off the charge and you will be indebted to him, and the ball is in your court. Of course, it is possible that your lawyer might be dazzlingly attractive but stupefyingly dumb and not be able to argue his way out of a paper-bag in which case you'll be banged up in chokey and the only male you'll have any chance of getting off with is Lord Longford.

Be careful though of trying the "Je m'accuse" ploy. If the police cotton on to what you have done, they may well arrest you for wasting police time. Invite the Chief Constable to the wedding.

If all this seems a little too far-fetched, you can always get yourself invited to dinners at the Inns of Court. These are smart occasions, but the food is truly lousy, so you may not think you can stomach it. If you can, make sure you have a pair of shoes that are easily removed, and you must sit next to your intended victim. Play footsie with him a little, and then exclaim in a loud and shocked voice, that someone is playing footsie with you, and surely you cannot be the intended recipient of said foot - and look with narrow eyes at the girl on the other side of the table. The lawyer will be so worried about the other woman trying to man hunt that you will have his complete and uninterrupted attention. Do make sure though, that you have put your shoes back on.

You could always ask to see him for legal reasons or because you are interested in writing a thesis on his special subject. You have to be obvious. Subtlety is not a strong point with them because they are trained only to look at the facts before them.

Sitting on his desk and fluttering eye lashes takes nerve, and it is much easier just to ask him to lunch with you so that you can discuss your thesis/your case with him. Make sure you book a restaurant that has a hotel upstairs or nearby.

Bribe his secretary into changing all his appointments in the afternoon (secretaries rather approve of man hunters - lawyers aren't very good at looking after themselves) with a bottle of champagne or perfume, and use all your feminine guile and Wonderbra throughout lunch. It is worth knowing that most lawyers consider themselves incorruptible, so they don't tend to drink at lunch time. Of course, any well mannered man will accompany a girl who drinks, and if he does, he's stuck. Lawyers have a tendency to get very drunk, but have too much of a reputation to uphold not to behave like gentlemen. Also, if he is anything of a gentleman and you really are writing a thesis or are able to create a good enough sob story for him, he will pay for lunch.

Where To Look

Best places to select your lawyer are the Legal Five Hundred, a guide that comes out every year with the top 500 legal firms and their specialisations. Each law firm is required to list its partners in order of seniority at reception, so look at the top 12 names.

Otherwise it is worth hanging out in smart but old fashioned restaurants - Simpsons, Wiltons or the Savoy.

You could always find yourself some high roller somewhere they always have a lawyer somewhere in their entourage - but you may prefer the roller anyway.

As a last resort you can bump off a relative who intends to leave you some money, and wait for the will to be read. If said rich uncle has not left you anything, contest.

What to Wear

You must be well dressed, but again labels really don't matter. His first appraisal of you is going to be whether you can afford to pay his fees.

Of course, this is never going to become an issue,

but he doesn't know that. As explained, the lawyer you are after works very hard, so he will be delighted a little sex appeal will jolt him into lust. The little black number with paste, pearls and padding will usually do the trick. However, this is not recommended in the daytime.

Problem areas:

He may always start to suspect you of being guilty of a crime - and you probably will be.

He has an analytical mind and may even realise that he is being hunted. If he asks you your motives, do your best to avoid answering - he has a way of cross-examining, and finding out whether you are telling the truth or not. And we all know the truth is his actual or potential bank balance.

He will never talk about his work. He's not allowed to. This means that he is used to being secretive, and it is difficult to tell if he is being hunted by anyone else.

Pick-Up Lines

"Which would you recommend for a poor little innocent like me, 1963 Warre's or 1961 Taylor's?"

"Is that a writ you just dropped or am I unlucky?"

"Without prejudice against what?"

THE JESUS FREAK

Well there has to be something to do in church for the non-believer, and that thing is looking around the congregation.

It is always best to sit near the front of the church to do this, because it is easier to judge a person by his face than by the back of his head (though it is useful to know whether he has dandruff or a bald patch before you finally make your choice). Of course it is rather off-putting for the vicar reading out the sermon that took him three weeks to write on the subject of "The Church and the Sexual Revolution" to see someone in the front pew is not only paying no attention but actually has her back to him and is making hand-signals that only a bookie could understand to his curate.

The Jesus Freak is the beatific one, who will either be sitting, at the most, two rows behind you, or will be in front of you in the choir (or pulpit). The classic way of trapping your Jesus Freak is to offer to teach Sunday School, drop your hymnal and prayer book when close to him, or even a handkerchief. Dropping your knickers won't work - he tends to be far too proper to appreciate this gesture.

A Jesus freak is not a bad catch, and is not too challenging for a beginnner in man hunting. He will generally be clean, honest and decent. A mite dull perhaps, but then what do you expect from someone who eats fish every Friday, knows why people eat pancakes on Shrove Tuesday and complains that the meaning has gone out of Christmas. He may give off an unnerving whiff of incense but this will be as nothing to the odour of sanctity he will exude. Worse than Virginia Bottomley closing down a hospital.

But he does have bread and wine for breakfast once a week, and spends a fair proportion of his day on his knees, and that's no bad thing. A word of warning - one of the greatest choruses in Handel's Messiah starts "And we like sheep".

The quickest way to pick up a Jesus Freak is to dab red nail varnish onto the palms of both hands and blush modestly as he says: "How interesting. Stigmata".

Other Types

Other types of Jesus Freaks (aka Moonies, Mormons, Seventh Day Immersionists, Hare Krishnas - not to be confused with Hare Carpenters) are easy to find, but are best avoided. If you are really desperate to extend you man hunt to this section of religious lunatic, it is best to move to America (and stay there).

Hermits are hard to find, and even leaving little dishes of milk out for them at night is not guaranteed to work. You may end up with a hedgehog rather than a hermit. In the eighteenth and nineteenth centuries, hermits were paid by the grandees on whose land they lived, at the end of their five or 10 year seclusion. This does not happen any longer, as most hermits might now be considered tramps, so it is not really worth hunting them. They are penniless when they are hermits, and will have no pay-off at the end.

Where To Look

To find this type of Jesus freak, get a copy of Pevsner, and look through for the best churches in the area. Even if you don't like the look of the choice of men you are faced with, you will enjoy the architecture.

There are other places to find your man than church, or the Methodist Hall. You could try confirmation classes or even choirboy practices, though you may find your prey a little immature.

There are plenty of do-gooders at the local jumble sale and the village fete always seems to be opened by the local vicar.

What To Wear

A hat and gloves - the Henley look - always go down well on Sundays - but try to look demure. You don't want to scare him off. However, if you look as though you need help, are a little down at heel and your hems are coming down, he may come to look after you.

Problems

It is not worth hanging around any of the Jesuit

schools, Catholic colleges or the Vatican. All men of a decently huntable age in these areas are married to God or his mother. They do not fall into the happily or unhappily marrried man category, and there is not doubt that if you are successful with these guys you have committed a mortal sin.

You will always have to be good. This can be an unnerving experience for the best of us, but for a man hunter this is a problem indeed.

Imagine all those endless days cleaning the silver in church.

It is possible to be sinful but not heretical. You can burn the house down, go out with Hells Angels and pilfer the offertory box and he will always forgive you (cf. any novel by Joanna Trollope) but if you dare question any of the higher articles of faith (not belief in God because no modern priest believes in God these days) you'll get a good kicking: "What do you mean you don't 'get' transubstantiation? You Jensenist heretic! Verger, get the stake and the faggots..."

Pick-Up Lines

"So which altar wine is better, the one at St Peter's or the one at St Paul's?"

"Show me the way to a better life."

"Bless me for I have sinned."

"So what is the catechism anyway?"

"Would you like a nice cup of tea and a biscuit after the service, love?"

THE SELF IMPROVER

The Self Improver lacks education and is anxious to have this fact removed from his record. The Self Improver is likely have an unexciting full time job, but feels that he can live with that, as long as he is getting a degree in something indefinable like Social History from night classes or the Open University or the backs of match boxes.

Remember that this is the thing that keeps the Self Improver ticking - and that it takes not 3 or 4 but 7 years to get a degree on the OU. This means that your man is going to be deeply engrossed in his socio-economics for 7 years and then will be as completely self important as someone who just left university - but by then he will be too old to grow out of it.

Anyone who needs to improve themselves must be seriously lacking in their own confidence anyway, but if you feel up to nurturing him, he can be quite a catch - he will always "do well for himself" and "come a long way".

To meet your Self Improver, if you are based in London, you will have to find yourself a copy of Floodlight, the Self Improver's bible, and find the type of SI you are after. Having spoken about SI's in Social History and Social Economics, however, I do not necessarily recommend them. You will probably have more fun with a man who is being taught to use his hands - woodwork or carpentry, perhaps catering (chefs are usually very sensuous men, but more of that anon), for obvious reasons. Be wary, though of those who are being taught to use their bodies - never trust the sexuality of the man who has taken up ballet dancing or fencing - too much cut and thrust by half.

Asking for help with homework has been a trick that has been used since girls were first allowed to go to school, and it still leads to great possibilities and opportunities. Better, though, to bone up on any subject and offer help. If you are going to be a man hunter you may as well be a smart arse when dealing with a Self Improver - he will be more than impressed.

Taking the SI back to basics, and suggesting that you try studying biology together is really dull - I mean think of all those diagrams and those frogs with their stomachs hanging open (we are referring to dissecting subjects here and not Gerard Depardieu in "Green Card"), and the old school tricks of passing or catapulting notes in class or dropping ink on your rival seem a little passe once you pass the age of 14. Besides, the age of the ink pen, regrettably, seems to be almost over. Throwing your notes all over the floor just in front of him, and then bursting into tears because they are now in the wrong order will work, but it is far too wet for any true man hunter - it's only for sissies. Much better to take the lead and volunteer for yourself and your victim to work together on some project of your own - like looking for truffles under acorns in the oak woods together, and report back to the class in a month and a half. SI will not only be honoured to be asked by the brain box of the class, but you will be in charge - and that is so comforting.

Where To Look

Hang around Birkbeck College or the technical text book sections of the library. This will give you insight into what he is studying and what level he has reached. Avoid the "For Beginners" guys - they've got too long to go.

Take up some social/intellectual game like chess and play it in the pub opposite the college that he's attending. The self imporver, unlike the student, has a certain amount of money to spend. BUT LEARN TO LOSE.

What to Wear

Self Improvers have a way of forgetting about fashion

and chic, so there is no need to get out your glad rags to hunt them. Much better to get yourself two or three grungy outfits, flat shoes and some metal rimmed glasses, whether you need them or not.

Problem Areas

He may want to talk about sedimentary rocks or taxation for years and that can be very very dull.

Whatever ploy you try, he has to be at college on average twice a week, and he'll be doing homework, a thing the rest of us grew out of years ago.

Pick-Up Lines:

"Which class are you in? - Oh I'm in the one above."

"Is that your A+ Thesis that you've dropped on the floor, or am I just being flattering?"

"I've got a copy of this term's exam papers. Fancy a sneak preview?"

THE HOME IMPROVER

For those of you who have never quite worked out

how to hang a window blind, or think that grouting is something that grows in window boxes, that a washer is a little lady who comes in on Tuesdays and Fridays or that Polyfilla is bird food, the Home Improver is a very useful person to hunt.

He will fix your central heating, build you a decent kitchen, mend the conservatory, and even do the gardening. When you decide you have had your home improved as much as in necessary, and you begin to find his mastic more interesting than his conversation (and you will, I promise you), you can dispose of him and keep all the assets. He is not exactly going to get joint custody of the bathroom is he?

Where To Look

You will not find the home improver with his mates in the pub, nor in any other place where gregarious people meet. This is not because he is in fact a loner, for usually he is quite a sociable fellow, but because he is busy home improving. Your must draw him from the simple terraced house that he has improved to such an extent that it now looks like Schloss Neuschwanstein airlifted into a suburb of Barnet and beard him in the D.I.Y. shop.

The bimbo approach works well - choose your victim carefully (check what he's looking at - if he is interested in ironing board covers and pink lavatory seats, he is not for you however cute he may be - better to go for the man with his eye on the ride-on lawn mower, revving the throttle and shouting "More power! More power!") and ask him for his advice. All home improvers are pleased with their ability, and are delighted to be able to help ladies in distress. "Do you think these shears are best for my roses, or are they better designed for borders?" is a bit dull, but "What do think of this jacuzzi?" followed by "I suppose I ought to get the professional in to plumb it for me" has so much more promise in it for both of you "Which type of cement is easiest to use for the floor of my cellar?" simply does not have the same ring to it.

Other Places To Look
You can always unfix the washer round your taps and ask for a plumber - check the local plumbing

service shops first because you might get some fat cheek-bottomed jeans-wearer who has a fag sticking out of one side of his mouth. Building sites and skip hunting also have potential and at least you can have a good look for possible victims before you make your final choice. Don't try the local dump. There'll be nothing and noone of interest.

What to Wear

Show some cleavage and some leg. Whatever shape either is, it'll have the desired effect. Primness is counter-productive.

Problem areas:

You may not share his taste in the avocado bathroom suite, and do you really want a bidet?

Fitted kitchens are a little bit passe.

Once you've spent too much time in a jacuzzi your skin goes wrinkly.

Pick-Up Lines

"Which is better for my hollyhocks? Tomato food or Wondergro?"

"So just where would you put the spanner in this?"

"How about a nice glass of Chablis while you're working?"

THE SPORTSMAN

Sportsmen are always worth the chase. After all, they won't be prepared to hide, scared in the tree like a pheasant. If you are anything decent as a markswoman, he is also extremely easy to bag. (Then you can hang them from their necks - or ankles if they are harey [sic] - and pinch them once in a while to see if they have become tender enough, and whether they are ready to pluck!)

The country sportsman is very much like a city lad in his tastes in women - very simple and basic but with dirtier finger-nails.

You will need to be carefully dressed. Having sought him in his own environment, the shooting field or the country pub where the hunt meets, you must make the most of whatever assets you have, but not be altogether out of place - a Moschino dress does not work terribly well at the Old Bull or the Magpie and Stump, but let's face it, no man hunter worth her salt would wear an old Barbour and an Alice Band.

Again, it is important to have some sort of understanding of the sport -a maiden in cricket, while it may be something that every bowler aspires to, does not necessarily refer to his woman. The ins and outs of the sport have nothing to do with sex . A guffaw and "Did you really throw a six?" might confuse a poor simple cricketer into thinking you suffer from dyslexia, when actually you thought that everyone who wears white plays backgammon.

It seems that every medium sized village in the country, especially in Yorkshire, fields its own cricket team - mostly composed of Graphic Designers who drive up from London for the weekend, thick-eared and drooling yokel psychopaths of the "Straw Dogs" variety and one weak-chinned priest who thinks playing cricket helps him "relate to the community". It is best to find yourself a cricketer who is a little better than village standard. Check local papers for the dates, times and places of the matches and sit or stand as close to the pavilion as possible. Do not disturb the cricketer when he is going out to be In but attract his attention when he is coming in after being Out. The glass of Pimms and sympathy technique works well, as does a request to explain why the umpire declared him out for such a great shot - after all it was his bat that hit the wicket, not the ball.

Rugby players are game for anything, but any man hunter must be aware that the likelihood is that a player of this sport will take on a rather rugged look, with the number of broken noses, and fingers directly in proportion to how good he is at the sport. Therefore the most proficient player always has the appearance of a dazed warthog. Do remember that the more broken the appendages, the less sensitive they are.

However, rugby boys tend to have something to hold on to, a great capacity for drink, and eat enough to put a family of Great Danes to shame. They are a little laddish, but this is only to be expected - they put their arms round parts of each other during the game, which would seem quite peculiar in any other circumstance, and then they all shower or bathe together afterwards. Rugby club jokes and stories are often the coarsest that you will ever encounter, but it is only their form of ribaldry. They are often genuinely scared of women, and so if you are interested in one, you may find you have to take on the whole rugby club to get to him. This is not recommended. However, joining the rugby supporters club, and going to the odd rugby dinner can be fun. Ask your intended victim about a particularly grappling tackle, and then show no comprehension in his description. Ask him for a demonstration, making sure that you are the tackler and he is the tackled. He will then be at your feet - always a good place to find any man.

If a footballer is what you are after, think again. Do you really want a man who drinks lager, kisses his fellows and cries in the corner? We think not.

Where To Look

In the gym, squash court, village green.

Get enthusaistic about your local team, and go to

watch the matches.

Hang out in the local sports shops, or find yourself a job selling gum shields or jock straps.

What to Wear

Something sporty or something that makes you look sporty will help. If not, you can always try wearing the team colours. This should be a good enough disguise.

Problem Areas

Do you really fancy washing his sweaty T-shirts or a jock strap? And what if he expects you to join him in a little exercise? He may be cute but some things are just beyond the pale.

Pick-Up Lines

"What sort of exercise do think would be best for my bottom, the bicycle or the skipping rope?"

"Ooh can I touch your biceps, I think they are just gorgeous."

"Do you want a suck of my Lucozade?"

LIFEGUARDS

They're hunky, they're fit and they're mostly gay. We all know how to get their attention. Try drowning (but do it in a swimming pool - it's so much easier to see you and they won't leave it till too late). Do not forget, though, that you never can tell who else he might have resuscitated mouth to mouth recently.

Where to meet them.

In water.
You could try doing a life saving class - but that would mean having to mouth to mouth a dummy, and I've never come across a woman who liked kissing a rubber doll.

What to Wear

As little as possible. Why leave anything up to their imagination if you don't have to?

Waterproof mascara and kissable lipstick.

A decent tan and hair extensions.

Pick-Up Lines

"Help!"
"Glug."

Problem Areas

He's always going to be at least as beautiful as you and, if you let that bottom slip, there'll always be someone else's whose hasn't.

His tan will always be better, even if it's fake. You never know who he will lie on top of his body tomorrow, and he has been snoggong a rubber lady.

THE NEW AGE HIPPY

Now searching for one of these in his natural environment would be extremely unpleasant. Many of these types of men live in the camp sites reserved for them (they are otherwise known as travellers, but don't go looking at the club of that name).

It is much better to seek him out where he may not be amongst his peers, or at least in mixed company.

Where to find him

Come across a strong scent of goat, then follow it to its source.

Take up yoga, herbal massage or the local vegetarian pressure group, and there he will be.

What to Wear

You will need a certain amount of specialist equipment, because the New Age Hippy has a different understanding of camouflage. You will have to invest in two bar open toed sandals and a nicely tie-dyed dress. Hindu beads come in quite useful and it is essential to have a couple of hair wraps plaited in to your hair. If it is too short, buy a wig (natural hair of course). You must not wear make-up; your perfume should be something frightfully PC from the Body Shop.

Problem Areas

Your hippy will completely believe that he is on the same wavelength as you. Actually, though, he is quite easy prey and not a bad catch, but only for a

very short time. It doesn't take long before you will become either
1 - Sick of hearing about his aura man,
2 - Find that none of your usual companions are speaking to you,
or 3 - Worst of all, that you realise that you have spent three weeks without washing your hair and what an uplifting (and down greasing) experience it is.

Pick-Up Lines

"This is great, man",

"Can you put me in touch with my inner self, man?"

"It's in the power of the stars, man."

"Do you think I am more Ying or more Yang?"

"Are these your worry beads or was it a lucky find?"

"Why did Kurt Cobain have to die?" (Anyone who's ever listened to a Nirvana album will know the answer to that one).

THE HAPPILY MARRIED MAN

For a man hunter, the married man is the great white whale of catches and, as with any large game fishing, ninety-nine times out of one hundred, the line will break once the fish has taken the bait.

They tend to have a great many reasons to stay as they are, and so are not necessarily likely to take part in the chase. This is because they have been caught once already. However, if you get them at the ideal time - after the rutting season - it tends to be a little easier.

Looking for married man while his erstwhile hunter is still on heat can be very difficult indeed, but this situation does not carry on for ever. The only time that he is truly obvious is when he is on the church or registry steps, and this is perhaps not the ideal time to hunt.

Married men, especially men who might otherwise have the tendency to stray, are kept under wraps by their original hunters, who are extremely territorial. Do not forget, however, that all men are fair game.

The bait for a happily married man must be something he does not get at home, and the strategy must be simple but effective. The easiest way of getting your married man is to find yourself working for him or in the same department as him and fell him over a drink. But this is old hat, and the others working with you will warn him of a female predator. Much better is to take the masculine role in the situation. Visit the same restaurant as he does and watch his behaviour pattern.

If he drinks or if he cracks a joke with his companions (and they have to be male) send a glass of champagne and a bowl of strawberries with your card. Make sure that the waiter gives it to the right man though, because otherwise you might be stuck with some geek with a bald patch and the rest of his hair swept over the top to hide it. I have never known a man send a glass of champagne back, and there is something rather exciting for a man to vamped by a woman. He will always say that he is happily married and that it is time he left, but if you come up with a good story, like you've been stood up, any decent sort of man will accompany you home.

Making the first move takes guts but throws the man off balance and also leaves you in the position of power - ooh, and there are so many good things that come to those in a position of power.

Where else to look

If your intended victim is not quite that sophisticated, and you don't feel up to the challenge of exposure quite yet, you could always try the irresistible technique. Hang around his watering holes, or find yourself a regular seat opposite him in the train, wear suspenders and a little lost look and if he does not come around to eating out of your hand very quickly, try the next man.

You will need a full train timetable for this, as well as a guide to hotels with quiet restaurants.

Happily married men are not embarrassed to be seen with another woman, because they are happily married. Remember that this means he is approachable.

You could always try working for him (or, which is better, have him work for you). Then, when you get bored, you can have him up for sexual harassment.

The other, and rather wayward, ploy is to pretend to be hunting someone else, and ask him what he thinks would be best in the circumsatances ("What shade of lipstick do you think suits me better?")

What to Wear
Look sophisticated and clean, but a little wanton. Remember that he thinks he has it all already, and you have to knock him slightly off-balance.

Problem Areas
Well these are pretty obvious. A huge loyalty to his wife. You will be turning him in to a deceitful and possibly unhappily married man. There is a bitter-sweetness to this, rather like losing your virginity.

Pick-Up Lines
"Which of these presentations do you think works better?"

"Is that a hotel key that you dropped or was it just a

lucky find?"

"I know you've got to get home, but how about a quick drink. It's been a very tough day".

THE UNHAPPILY MARRIED MAN

Not too hard to find. Almost all men who are married are unhappy. So are almost all women.

This is easy prey - do not believe lines like "My wife doesn't understand me and all I need is a little tender loving care". Take him for all he's worth, but remember that you may well be cited in the divorce proceedings. Unhappily married wives are always looking for someone to blame. It is never their fault, but they would probably rather blame the man hunter rather than the man.

All you need for the unhappily married man is to look something like the woman he first married (or thought he first married), because an unhappily married man is always still a bit in love with his wife.

If you hang around his corner of the bar/pub/office/club he will end up talking to you, and will think that he has struck gold. If he doesn't approach you, the oldest line in the book works wonders - it could have been designed for him - "Do you come here often?" Be charming, sensitive, warm and even sincere if you must. Remember, though, that half of the Porsche that he is driving probably belongs to his wife, and his wife's presence will be with you wherever you are, checking how much he is spending on you. It will affect her alimony.

Unhappily married men are not the easiest people to spot, though they do tend to have a hangdog look about them when they think that there is nobody looking. However, you will not find it too difficult to find him - we all know one, and he'll probably approach you anyway, because we all know that you are wonderful. You will need, however, an excellent restaurant guide to the area in which you live, or the place you visit for your dirty weekends. It is better to spend the money before the divorce than afterwards.

What to Wear

It really doesn't matter too much. If you can't look like his wife, just wear stockings and false eyelashes (and something in between if you must). Wearing a little sympathy and loads of loving care is essenntial though.

Where To Find Him

Playing squash at 8 pm, or working late in the office. Have a breakfast meeting - this will ensure that he has had to leave his wife very very early in the morning and, if he is a borderline case, he'll soon be an unhappy one. You'll also find him hanging around the London clubs late on a Thursday or Friday, but that unhappy man is rather desperate. Probably best to leave him alone.

Problem Areas

Whatever happens, it'll all be your fault, and in the end he actually loves his wife really.

Pick-Up Lines

"What do you think would suit a single girl better a holiday on a beach on the Greek Islands or walking the Atlas mountains?'

"Oh you're married? God that must be awful"

"You look as though you need a drink".

THE OLDER MAN

There are better ways of finding yourself an older man than hanging around the geriatric wards in the hospital. After all, you may want an older man, but you don't want one who dribbles, has bed sores, who can't make it to the lavatory on his own. He would have to be rich - no, very rich, - and terminally ill for that to be worth it. Slightly younger older men are probably more fun to be with. Of course the one that you are hunting is gentlemanly and charming (and they are not all, believe me). He will also be reasonably well off, having settled to his rightful place in the world. You will not have to struggle with huge ambition, and mortgages will be a thing of the past. The disadvantages are big, but not insurmountable. You may have to put up with yet another story about the war, and the "Life isn't what it used to be when I was your age" chorus can become a real drag. It is sensible to arm yourself with a certain amount of foreknowledge of wines, and develop a taste for roast beef. It is also worth reading up in one of the books on D Day or the

Normandy landings. You are bound to be quizzed on it.

The art of conversation is very important to older people. After all, they cannot be as active as they wished they once were, and if your going to get your pants off one way or the other, you may as well let them do it by boring you. They will think you are amazingly good company. An older gentleman appreciates small gestures, such as offering to help him across the road.   Even is he is not yet ancient, he will take it as a mark of respect

Where to find him

First of all, you must find yourself in an area where the likelihood of finding your pensioner is high. Eastbourne and Torquay are reasonably good; Madeira is better if you can afford it, but the perfect place is one of the stuffy London clubs. The Reform or the Travellers are ideal. Or the Youth Programming Department of BBC 2.

What to Wear

You must be well dressed, but not necessarily showing too much leg. You do not want to give the old codger a heart attack.

Problem Areas

He will bore you half the time. He never found out where the washing machine was. He has probably written his will already and is only looking for a bit of fluff. It is, in fact, essential that you take over his office work to find out if this is so. And that's boring again.

Pick-Up Lines

"Hello, dear. Can you hear me. If you want my body, just nod. Aren't you marvellous for 83?".

"Which do you recommned for my liver complaint - Earl Grey or Lapsang?

"Is this your Cod Liver Oil, or was it just a lucky find?"

"Don't I recognise you from somewhere" or "Haven't I seen your face somewhere before?" works a dream. An older man is always proud of his achievements, and he will suggest three or four possible situations to which you may be referring.

THE NEW MAN

If your ideal is a man who wears the apron around the house, then the p.c. way of describing him is the New Man. He is a caring, sharing sort of a person who is kind to stray dogs and cats. He is without great driving ambition, or great driving anything else for that matter, and when you say you are tired, have a headache or a hangover, instead of admonishing you he will "Understand" and try to administer care. He will read the women's problems pages in magazines, so that he knows how to cope with you better, and then quote them at you. He will, however, be clean, polite and rather sweet.

Where to find him

New Men do not congregate - if they did it would probably be at an ironing (or should that be pressing) conference, but there are ways of finding him. He will work in counselling, social services or the dole office. He will more than likely have studied ESP so that he can help people before they know their problems. Losing your job is a sure fire way of bumping into one, but this is not to recommended. Joining a major, worthy charity organisation will probably give you more choice, though.

You could always hang around the Oxfam shop or the bottle bank. New Man recycles.

What to Wear

It helps to look disorganised and slightly dishevelled - you must look as though he would have a useful role to play for you. New Man likes to be beneficial to his companion, and it can be a great pleasure to use him. Look hungry, and say that your cooker is broken, and he will offer to cook for you, faint, and he will nurse you, share a taxi and he will pay.

Problem Areas

He's just too nice. He's no fun to tease, he'll say he enjoys it. Ugh. You'll want to knock some sense into him. He'll like that too.

He'll never tell you what to do - he'll always say it's up to you. You know that anyway. It should be refreshing but it isn't.

Pick-Up Lines

"Mow my lawn".

"Cook supper".

"Shut up".

MEN YOU SHOULDN'T HUNT

Insolvents - These men are hard to spot, but once you have recognised one, all the others will become obvious. They are very good at drinking other people's champagne and are always at other people's parties. If they are any good at their indebtedness, they will be extremely charming - and you do not want them around you - you'll find them extremely tenacious whenever you have a cheque book or an American Express to hand.

Men with small feet - they will tell you that there is no truth in the rumour about men with small feet, and how the same is said to be true of men with small noses. Remember that it is much easier, and sometimes free, for the man concerned to have his nose fixed to look larger than his feet.

Badly dressed men - This is something that any male should have learnt by the time he has reached puberty. He does not have to be elegant or smart but, be honest, do you really want to be seen with someone who wears a shell suit or grey spongiform shoes

French men - they never heard of hygiene. Can you consider yourself successful at hunting if you find yourself with a man who smells of vile French cigarettes and eats garlic in bed?

Social climbers - They will sniff at anything better than them like a dog. That of course includes you. They can be amusing company, because they are always eager to impress, so once they've found you they will lavish you with gifts and, until they find someone one step up the ladder.

.....If all else fails, stand on a street corner near Paddington and wear little more than hot pants and welcoming smile.

A word of caution to all of you who finally master the fine art of man hunting. As with any sportswoman, once you have succeeded, it is necessary to find something a little bit tougher. The natural progression of man hunter leads to man eater and, to misappropriate Oscar Wilde, this is the unspeakable in full pursuit of the uneatable .

MANHUNTING - TROUBLESHOOTING

The last section of this book deals with "troubleshooting". Or, in other words, what you should do when something goes wrong. And, you better believe it, something will certainly always go wrong. As night follows day, as pain follows pleasure, as Conservative MPs follow secretaries into the broom closet, whatever can go wrong, will go wrong.

But don't panic. From the smouldering of disaster can be plucked the burning jewel of victory - so long as the manhunter in question has courage, wit and fingers of asbestos. Even the most disasterous situations - ie. you turning up at a man's office's costume party as Mammy from "Gone With The Wind" only to find his boss' wife is black - can be turned to your advantage. Somehow.

The key is to see disaster coming and interdict it as

quickly as possible. The first inkling that something is wrong is intuitive. If your sixth sense tells you that things aren't going according to plan, go with it. If you're in a BA Airbus 40,000 feet over the Arctic icecap and you think one of the engines is making a funny noise, then go ahead and tell the stewardess. Don't be frightened of making a fool of yourself. You're going to look a lot more foolish sitting on your slowly sinking luggage in the middle of the Barents Sea amidst floating wreckage 2000 miles from the nearest habitable igloo and nothing to eat but your lipstick.

But sometimes, with the best will in the world, disaster strikes without warning. Sure, you might have been able to warn the aircrew on your plane that No.1 engine's spluttering sound was not a healthy sign, but there was no way you could have known that the captain was going to emerge from the cockpit with an eerie faraway look in his eyes and say in a high-pitched sing-song voice: "Please Mr. Conductor, will you let me off at Piccadilly Circus, 'cos I'm only little?".
It is for these kind of situations that the following advice is given.

On Man Hunting In An Neighbourhood Of Markedly Lower Social Orientation

Keep walking.

On Manhunting In A Neighbourhood of Markedly Lower Social Orientation and Differing Ethnic Classification To Your Own.

Keep walking and keep smiling.

On Manhunting In Completely The Wrong Outfit.

You know what this is like. You've dolled yourself up to the nines. You've slipped into a glimmering silver lamé sheath and white stillettos. Your makeup is perfection. Your hair has that windswept look but with a natural hold. You walk into the party and... everyone's dressed as chickens. It's fancy dress and you misread the invitation.

In this particualr circumstance, you must immediately announce to the man you've got your eye on that you've just come from a much smarter, much more stylish party and just didn't have time to change. His large papier-maché beak will soon be nodding in appreciation.

Wearing the wrong outfit in the wrong circumstance is death to the inexperienced manhunter. It looks like you're trying too hard. So don't wear the spangly boob-tube and white pumps when invited beagling by a hunky hunstman or the twin-set and pearls when out picking up Class War Activists at your local riot.

When in doubt, there are two types of outfit in which you can go almost anywhere and do almost anything. By day, a charcoal grey two-piece business suit and, by night, a little black dress (of course if you are on the larger side and the little black dress will fit you about as adequately as a kleenex, then make it a large black dress). In these two outfits you can hunt men in places as diverse as a Sicilian funeral, the Le Mans 24 Hour Rally, besieged Sarajevo and *The Spectator* Christmas Party (and we assure you that you can find red-blooded males at all these venues - except, perhaps, the last one. But who knows? Jeffery Bernard might hop in).

Manhunting When You've Lost Your Hair

Chemotherapy, ring-worm, a tragic accident filimg a Pepsi commercial - after anyone of them, you could end up with your long, luxurious tresses on the floor, fit for nothing but stuffing a sofa.

Whatever you do, don't be tempted to "go bald". However much Sinead O'Connor, Hufty from "The Word" and Sigourney Weaver might argue, bald is not beautiful. You will look like nothing more than a billiard ball that's attracted a static coating of fluff.

And don't go for a wig either. These never work. Despite all the efforts of your hairdresser, they always look about as natural as a luminous prosthetic leg on a Tahitian cliff diver. And watch out for the cheaper attachments now available. The artifical fibres they employ are highly flammable. You might be at a smart restaurant, exchanging glances with the lads at the bar, when a waiter decides to light up the crepes suzette too close to your hair-do and suddenly your beehive turns into a scale model out of "The Towering Inferno".

If you have been so unfortunate as to lose your hair, wear a close fitting silk turban. It looks good, it's easy to wear and will give you a touch of the mystic orient

On Manhunting When You've Exposed A Little More Of Yourself Than You'd Planned

You're stepping out of the sportscar, the photographers flash-bulbs are popping, you extend one long, willowy leg, there's a ripping sound, and your skirt splits all the way up to the label of your Marks & Spencers knickers.

There's nothing you can do but laugh about it. Don't worry about your loss of dignity - be a good sport and go with it. Have a giggle along with anyone watching, give them a little twirl if necessary and then retire, at a brisk pace, to the nearest Ladies with needle and thread. Don't burst into tears, throw your handbag on the ground and have a fit of the screaming heeby-jeebies. This doesn't look good on the cover of "Hello".

Some situations can be guarded against. When you're dancing seductively in a tight, short Lycra number in some crowded nightclub and you trip over your heels, spin across the highly polished floor and up-end a waiter carrying a tray of Kahlua, your breasts will inevitably pop out of your dress. Ah, but you are ready - there is a strong case to be said for pasting large gold, paper stars over both nipples. Yes, this might be uncomfortable but if your upper bodywork is ever inadvertently exposed and menfolk find themselves gazing at your heavenly body, they will certainly be intrigued to find themselves staring at two glistening stars. And they will ask themselves - what kind of private life does this girl lead? And arousing curiosity is the first step in becoming a successful manhunter.

Remember that, girls.